treasured moments

treasured moments
on cape cod & the islands

photography by Dan Ford

PARACLETE PRESS

BREWSTER, MASSACHUSETTS

10 9 8 7 6 5 4 3 2 1

©2001 by Daniel B. Ford, Jr.
ISBN 1-55725-279-3

Cover design by Sarah Andre
Interior design by Sarah Andre and Hans Spatzeck-Olsen

Published by Paraclete Press
Brewster, Massachusetts
www.paracletepress.com

Printed in Singapore.

Year after year, many people are drawn back to Cape Cod and the Islands. Others have moved here to live year-round. These people have discovered unique places that have a special meaning for them: an inlet, a quiet marsh, a spectacular overlook of the breaking surf, or a beautiful pond that's impossible for the first-time visitor to find. Some treasure the image of the split-rail fence following a dirt road that disappears over a knoll; others prefer the scene of a dory nestled next to a dock. These locations are special for different reasons. Regardless of the place—the view—that evokes nostalgia, the common denominator is that it touches something in our hearts. To each one of us it's peace, it's vacation, it's a part of life that ranks up there—way up there—with the angels and the big blue sky.

And that's what this book is about: Cape scenes that bring back memories and produce a warm feeling inside . . . and make us smile.

For as long as I can remember I've loved looking—on bright, sunny days—at scenery. At first, I looked out the back window of my parents' car as we moved rapidly through the country-side (my father was a fast driver). I'd frame the scenes in my mind and crop them to simplify the "picture" and enhance its beauty. And now, well, I'm still doing the same thing only with a camera to record the scene, and on a piece of land that's very special—Cape Cod.

Dan Ford

about the photographer:

Dan Ford's love for photography, although apparent through college years and his military service, was never commercial until 1978, when he started The Ford Collection, a firm established to market his photographic landscape scenes.

Prior to this, Ford spent nineteen years with one of the country's largest industrial real estate firms, rising to become its president. In 1975, he moved with his wife and family (three children) to an ecumenical Christian community on Cape Cod. There, he gained a new-found perspective that enabled him to see and capture on film the serenity and quiet joy of overlooked nooks and tranquil vistas. It wasn't long before his photographs, matted and framed, started appearing in offices, conference rooms, and reception areas of major corporations throughout the country.

Now, several years after his retirement, Ford is at it again. All of us who have a love for the Cape are delighted that he has once again loosed his camera to bring to life many of those treasured scenes that make Cape Cod and the Islands so special.

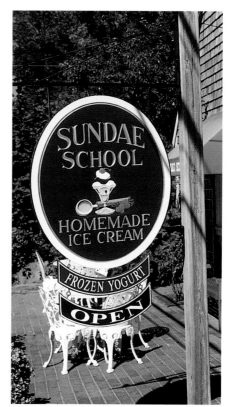